19.95

Ripley's Believe It or Not!

Developed and produced by Ripley Publishing Ltd

This edition published and distributed by:
Mason Crest Publishers Inc.
370 Reed Road, Broomall, Pennsylvania 19008
(866) MCP-BOOK (toll free)
www.masoncrest.com

Ripley's Believe It or Not!
Extraordinary Animals
ISBN 978-1-4222-1533-3
Library of Congress Cataloging-in-Publication data is available

Ripley's Believe It or Not!—Complete 16 Title Series
ISBN 978-1-4222-1529-6

PUBLISHER'S NOTE
While every effort has been made to verify the accuracy of the entries in this book,
the Publishers cannot be held responsible for any errors contained in the work.
They would be glad to receive any information from readers.

WARNING
Some of the stunts and activities in this book are undertaken by experts and should not
be attempted by anyone without adequate training and supervision.

Printed in the United States of America

Ripley's Believe It or Not!®

EXTRAORDINARY ANIMALS

RIPLEY PUBLISHING

a Jim Pattison Company

Extraordinary Animals

is a collection of fascinating tales about a
brood of crazy creatures. Read about a
snake with two heads, a chameleon whose
tongue can extend one and one half times
its body length, and a woman who lived
in a glass box with 3,400 scorpions—all in
this incredible book.

Visitors to Stockholm Zoo in Sweden are allowed to
get really close to the resident spiders...

Deep and Deadly Bite

The viperfish has over 350 light organs on its body to attract fish in the dark depths where it hunts.

The viperfish's teeth protrude far beyond its mouth and eyes. To scale, if your teeth were this big, they would stick out an amazing 12 in (30 cm)! It has the longest teeth, in proportion to its head, of any animal.

This monster fish is one of the fiercest predators of the deep. To attract its prey it has a long dorsal spine with a light-producing tip. It is thought that the viperfish approaches its victims at high speed, impaling them on its teeth, extending its hinged skull to swallow large prey.

TOP FIVE
BRIGHTEST FISH

More than 1,500 kinds of fish glow or shine to lure prey and attract mates. Some can be seen from 98 ft (30 m) away.

1 **Flashlight fish**
2 **Lanternfish**
3 **Dragonfish**
4 **Slickhead**
5 **Midshipman**

Slimeball The world's slimiest animal must surely be the hagfish. It sheds a sticky substance from its skin that mixes with seawater to make a mass of slimy mucus ten times the volume of the fish itself.

Scavenger Hagfish have the slimiest habits too. They use their sucker-like mouths to bore into decaying carcasses, then live inside the dead animal as it rots away.

Flashdance A flashlight fish's light organs act like headlamps. By blocking off these lights and changing direction in the dark, it can confuse predators.

LIKE MOTHS TO A FLAME
Lanternfish use their bodily light (photophores) to attract both their prey, which comprises smaller fish, and also to attract a mate at breeding time. Some males and females have different patterns, allowing them to recognize each other in dark water.

Never seen Alive Beaked whales are champion divers, staying underwater for two hours or more. Most kinds are rare—Longman's beaked whale has never been seen alive and is known only from two washed-up skulls.

At 65 ft (20 m) long and 60 tons in weight, the bull sperm whale is the world's biggest predator. One was found with an entire 40-ft (12-m) long giant squid in its stomach! This gigantic specimen was stranded and died on Roemoe Island in the North Sea in 1997.

COOL HEAD

As the sperm whale comes up from a dive, its head "melts"! The forehead contains about 25 bathtubfuls of the substance spermaceti. This turns hard and waxy in the cold depths, then expands and becomes more oily as the whale rises again.

Take a Breath When a whale breathes in, it sucks about 500 gal (2,000 l) of air within about 2 seconds!

BOTTOM FIVE

DEEPEST-DIVING MAMMALS

1 Sperm whale
9,900 ft (3,000 m) plus

2 Bottlenose whale
6,500 ft (2,000 m)

3 Killer whale
3,300 ft (1,000 m)

4 Elephant seal
2,300 ft (700 m)

5 Weddell seal
1,970 ft (600 m)

The giant squid can grow to a massive 66 ft (20 m)—that's almost as long as a tennis court! It has the world's biggest eyes. Larger than soccer balls, they help it to see flashes of light that are made by its prey of fish and smaller squid, at its favorite hunting depth of up to 3,000 ft (1,000 m).

"*swallows prey weighing ten times more than itself*"

SICKENING TRICK

Sea-cucumbers are relatives of starfish and sea urchins. They live in deep waters and tidal pools and sift mud for edible scraps. In some regions they are the most common dwellers of the ocean floor. If disturbed, they throw up —ejecting not only feces, but also particles of decayed food and mud over their attacker. The slimy discharge contains much of their guts, which look like pale threads.

The largest animal mouth, compared to body size, belongs to the gulper eel (pelican eel). This weird fish, 24 in (60 cm) long, extends its jaws to swallow prey weighing ten times more than itself.

In Pieces A type of sponge, called the red sponge, incredibly can break into thousands of pieces—without dying! The broken pieces of the animal reform until it is whole again.

KISS OF LIFE

In the vast black ocean depths it can take time to find a breeding partner. When the tiny male deep-sea anglerfish mates, he grabs the larger female with his mouth, hangs on, and gradually joins or fuses with her body so that he can never leave. He even shares her food via her blood supply, and, in return, fertilizes her eggs.

Back in the Swim Again The 5 ft (1.5 m) fish, the coelacanth, thought to have died out with the dinosaurs, caused a sensation when discovered alive and well by scientists off south-east Africa in 1938. Exactly 60 years later the same thing happened in Indonesia, when another, different species of coelacanth was found.

Longest Survivor The title "greatest living fossil" goes to the lampshell or lingula. It looks like a clam but is a separate animal group that has survived for more than 450 million years.

Octopuses can learn to count to five and even distinguish different shapes! Apart from dolphins, they are the cleverest sea creatures—this octopus has been taught to open closed jars in order to grab hold of the small crabs inside.

Killer Shark

The huge, serrated, triangular teeth of the great white shark are amazingly adapted for tearing into flesh! It often swims along with teeth bared, just to warn other sharks to keep away from its territory.

Great whites are fast learners, and some develop the habit of cruising just off beaches, waiting for unwary swimmers. A "small" great white caught off Japan in 1954 had swallowed a 13-year-old boy— whole!

The great white attacks ferociously, retreats while the injured prey becomes weaker, and then returns to gorge on the flesh!

The movie Jaws (U.S. 1975) was based on a rogue shark that terrorized beaches on Long Island, and killed at least five people in the summer of 1916. The most likely culprit, which had the shin of a boy in its stomach when caught, was probably not a great white but a bull shark.

Bitten in Half

Australian diver and shark expert Rodney Fox needed 462 stitches during a four-hour operation after a shark attack. He was nearly bitten in half, and his abdomen was fully exposed with all his ribs broken on the left-hand side of his body. He was rushed to the hospital—only held together by his wet suit! Just three months later, he was back in the water with his own personal memento—a great white tooth embedded in his wrist.

Rodney Fox was ferociously attacked in 1963 by a great white shark during a spear-fishing tournament off Aldinga Beach, Australia—and survived to tell the tale!

Dangerous Waters In South America, people swimming or even washing their clothes have been bitten and killed by bull sharks that have swum up the Amazon, 1,500 mi (2,500 km) inland.

EATEN ALIVE

Sharks attacked and killed more than 500 men in 1942 during World War II. A German submarine torpedoed a British ship carrying Italian prisoners-of-war off the coast of South Africa—all the men on board either drowned or were killed by the sharks.

The whale shark is the world's biggest fish, weighing in at more than 15 tons. Although five adults could fit into its cavernous mouth, fortunately it only eats minute plankton.

Not Fussy The tiger shark is called the "garbage can shark" because it bites and swallows almost anything—edible or not. Tiger sharks have been cut open to reveal swallowed fuel cans, bicycle tires, lumps of wood, parts of a dead dog and in one, a tom-tom drum bigger than a soccer ball.

Largest Fish Ever Caught! A whale shark measuring 45 ft (14 m) in length, 23 ft 9 in (7 m) round its girth, and weighing 30,000 lb (13,600 kg) was captured after a fight lasting 39 hours at Knights Key, Florida, on June 1, 1912.

Pet Monster Hawaiian Tom K. Maunupau from Honolulu rode a 6-ft (2-m) shark that he kept as a pet!

Back to the Sea A dead shark sinks so slowly that its body is almost completely dissolved by the salt water before it reaches the bottom of the sea. The only part of the shark that is impervious to the action of the salt is its teeth.

Baby Teeth The tiger shark bears live young and may give birth to as many as 27 infant sharks, all perfectly formed and equipped with teeth.

Growing Smaller The paradoxical frog of South America grows up to 10 in (25 cm) as a tadpole but shrinks to about 3 in (7 cm) long when adult!

Water Filter Basking sharks take in 400,000 gal (1,500,000 l) of water through their mouths every hour.

Give us a Wink The shark is the only fish that can blink its eyes.

Blubber Lips The megamouth shark has bathtub-sized lips that could suck you in whole. But this shark, which grows to 16 ft (5 m) long and almost 1 ton in weight, feeds on tiny creatures hundreds of feet down. It was once thought to have glow-in-the-dark lips, but this has not been proved!

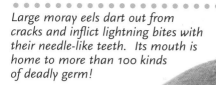

Large moray eels dart out from cracks and inflict lightning bites with their needle-like teeth. Its mouth is home to more than 100 kinds of deadly germ!

Sea Floor Builders Lamprey eels build nests 3 ft (10 m) high and 4 ft (1 m) wide on the bottom of the sea—both parents work together to carry heavy stones that make the nest.

Full of Air To ward off attackers, the globe-fish can inflate its body to three times its normal size by filling an air bladder inside its body.

Dangerous Jolts! The 220-lb (100-kg) Atlantic torpedo or electric ray sends out shocks of 200 volts, which could kill a person. In freshwater, the three-foot-long electric catfish generates 400 volts, while the electric eel delivers 500-plus volts, enough to knock out a horse.

Slippery Trip In New Zealand, blackwater rafting has become increasingly popular. The pastime involves riding inner tubes through dark, underground cave rivers that can be teeming with eels.

Ripley's ®

MEGALODON SHARK JAWS
EXHIBIT NO: 17583
JAWS BIG ENOUGH TO
SWALLOW A CAR

WAR IN THE WOMB!
The sand tiger shark grows its young in a womb-like part inside the body. The babies bite and fight inside the womb until the strongest one—usually the one that reaches a length of 2.5 in (60 mm) first—is left, having eaten the other babies. Some people have cut open pregnant sand tigers and had their fingers bitten by the unborn babies.

Ripley broadcasted a live radio show from the bottom of the shark tank at St. Augustine, Florida, on February 23, 1940.

Killer whales can weigh up to 10 tons and grow to 33 ft (10 m) in length—that's as big as a three-story building! There are only a few recorded attacks by killer whales on humans. They have at least 25 methods of hunting victims, including tipping penguins off ice floes. They also ride waves onto the shore and hurl themselves from the foam up the beach to grab an unwary seal. Then they wriggle around back into the water.

Sonic Attack Whale grunts are measured at 180 decibels. They are the loudest sounds made by any animal—about as loud as a rocket taking off. Sperm whales use their loud grunts to knock out prey.

Tune that Carries Humpback whales can sing for more than 20 hours non-stop. Their eerie moaning songs have been detected by underwater microphones from over 62 mi (100 km) away.

Hum Bug The 72-ft (22-m) fin whale's communication "song" is an immensely loud, low hum that has such a constant pitch that it has often been mistaken for throbbing ship engines. In 1964 a fin whale nearly caused a nuclear incident—U.S. sailors thought they heard a Russian attack submarine creeping into American waters.

ANTARCTIC PERIL

The first recorded fatality due to a leopard seal was in Antarctica in 2003 when a research scientist was attacked while snorkeling near the shore. The seal pulled the scientist under and she drowned. Leopard seals are big, fast, and fierce—over 13 ft (4 m) long and weighing in at half a ton.

Waterproof In the days of mass whaling, sailors cut off the foreskins of male great whales and used them as poncho-like raincoats.

TOP FIVE
WHALE PARASITES

Who'd want to be a whale? Many are infested with strange parasites that live on no other animal.

1 **Tapeworms** 98 ft (30 m) long in a sperm whale

2 **Lungworms** the size of a banana

3 **Lip lice** thumb-sized, not real lice (insect) but crab relatives

4 **Sinus flukes** leech-shaped, hand-sized animals in the sinus airways, occasionally burrow into the brain

5 **Barnacles** up to fist-sized, mainly on the head

The bowhead whale has the biggest head of any animal—one-third of its total body length! This whale was 53 ft (16 m) long with an 18-ft (5-m) long skull. Each lip measured over 33 ft (10 m) around the curve.

Poison in the Pool

The blue-ringed octopus may have a body that is only a little larger than a tennis ball, but it has a deadly bite, packing enough venom to kill at least seven people.

The blue-ringed octopus is usually dark brown. However, when it becomes agitated it turns a vivid yellow with electric blue rings.

In 1967 a man paddling in a rock pool in Australia lived only 90 minutes after being bitten. The blue-ringed octopus lurks in rock pools on the the coasts of the Indian and Pacific Oceans and bites people as they wander in the shallows. The bite itself may not be felt, but within five minutes or so the victim will become dizzy and have difficulty breathing.

Disarming The female nautilus, a deep-sea creature related to the octopus and squid, has about 90 arms.

All Eyes The deep-sea benthal octopus has eyes that are one-third the size of its entire body.

Struggle to Survive The female octopus gives birth to 200,000 offspring—but only one or two will reach maturity and reproduce themselves.

Fast Gain An octopus can increase its body weight by 2 percent a day.

Slow Loss In many species of octopus, the female is able to breed before she turns three years old, but she does so only once, dying soon after!

Land Grabs Some octopuses occasionally leave the water and crawl onto land to hunt for food. They can climb out of the water and up over rocks, or even walls.

Poor Crabs Octopuses have been known to climb over the edge of fishing boats and open up a hold full of crabs.

SALVAGE TOOL

A cargo of porcelain in a ship at the bottom of Japan's inland sea was recovered a century after the sinking. Octopuses like to curl up in confined spaces, so they were lowered into the wreckage and clung firmly to porcelain bowls and vases allowing them to be hauled safely back to the surface.

SUCKER FACTS

- An octopus has no skeleton and can "ooze" through an opening no bigger than its eyeball
- The octopus has three hearts, blue blood, and permanent high blood pressure
- The blue-ringed octopus usually only lives for two years
- Each octopus sucker can have up to 10,000 neurons (nerve cells) to help it touch and taste
- The pygmy octopus can live in one half of an empty clamshell, pulling the other half of the shell shut with its suckers
- Octopuses pass food from sucker to sucker into the hard beak within their mouth

SEA FACTS

- Many fish can change their sex
- Vampire snails crawl from the seabed at night to suck sharks' blood
- The Australian glass eel is so transparent that if you held it in front of these words you could easily read them
- Starfish feed by turning their stomach inside out through their mouth
- The giant ocean sunfish grows from the size of a pinhead to weigh more than 2 tons!

Quiet Life It is thought that some species of clams have lived for over 100 years.

Stung to Death In Australia a young boy died in less than five minutes after swimming into a swarm of jellyfish, called sea-wasps or box-jellies. He was allergic to the stings and his body couldn't cope with the poison.

The giant clam can weigh up to 500 lb (225 kg)—more than three average-size people! The shell opens and closes very slowly, and stories have been told of human-beings becoming trapped within its jaws!

Sex Flex Oysters are able to change from male to female and back again, depending on which is best for mating!

Suicide Fish The porcupine fish is so poisonous that it is often eaten in Japan as a means of committing suicide.

Seasonal Dish The Chinese fish of Australia is edible for nine months of the year, but poisonous in June, July, and August!

Deadly Beauty With a dark blue body and red teeth the trigger fish of Hawaii can be eaten safely, but when it is pale blue it is violently poisonous!

Last Step Stepping on the hollow spines of the laff fish's back can cause an extremely painful death to humans!

If a starfish loses an arm, it will grow another! Indonesian fishermen caught and chopped up starfish that were eating and ruining their shellfish beds. They threw the bits back into the water—and the starfish population rocketed because each of the arm parts grew into a new starfish.

TOP FIVE
STINGERS

These innocent-looking creatures can cause you intense pain if they sting you.

1 **Jellyfish** box-jellies and sea-wasps

2 **Sea urchins**

3 **Fire corals**

4 **Weever fish**

5 **Stonefish, lionfish**

Christmas Road Kill

A staggering 120 million red crabs crawl out of their burrows from the forest on Christmas Island and start their annual mating migration to the seashore. The route takes them through towns, highways, railroads, and cliffs to the sea.

About one million red crabs are killed every year crossing streets and railroad tracks on Christmas Island.

Revenge Ten times more people are stung by lionfish that are captive in aquariums, than by those in the wild. The sharp spines inject a poison causing an unbearable stinging pain.

LAND LOVER

The tree-climbing crab, which is commonly known as the robber or coconut crab, can grow to a width of 40 in (1 m) and weighs about 37 lb (17 kg). It lives mostly on land and, if submerged beneath the water for more than a few minutes, will drown.

Watery End The candiru, a parasitic fish of the Amazon, enters the body through the urethra and lodges itself in the bladder. It is fatal unless surgically removed quickly.

Deadly Spines The stonefish is said to have the most powerful poison of any sea animal and it can kill in 15 minutes. More than 50 deaths per year have been reported along coasts from India to Australia. The poison is injected by spines on the fish's back, as it lies camouflaged on a rock or is part-buried in sand.

Afterlife Men o'war and box-jellies can sting for many hours after being washed-up dead on the beach.

“bulls weigh up to five tons”

Elephant seals are as big as real elephants—the males weigh up to 5 tons. At breeding time they rear up and roar, and bite deep wounds in their rivals. They are so heavy that sometimes they trample or crush their own partners and offspring.

Mixed Family Female tortoises mate with several males at sea. One nest, therefore, can contain hatchlings that have different fathers.

TOP FIVE
SURVIVAL OF
THE FITTEST

Some sea animals can survive on land an amazingly long time.

1 **Robber crab**
2 **Climbing perch**
3 **Common eel**
4 **Mudskipper**
5 **Ghost crab**

Oily Resource Although a male elephant seal's blubber is just 7 in (18 cm) thick, it can yield as much as 210 gal (800 l) of oil!

Boring Shellfish The piddock shellfish slowly drills itself into solid rock by twisting its rough-surfaced shell to and fro. As it burrows it grows, so that it can never escape its stony prison. It feeds on tiny particles filtered from seawater.

Attack from the Rear One of the nastiest parasites on Earth is the parasitic barnacle. It lodges itself directly under a crab's tail and grows tentacles from its bag-like body into its host. It sucks out all the nutrients, eventually killing the crab!

Misleading Frills The king ragworm, up to 1.5 ft (0.5 m) long, has a frilly-edged body and looks harmless. Unlike most worms, it has a powerful bite and can easily draw blood.

WORLD'S LONGEST ANIMAL?

The longest creature is not a snake or even a whale—it's the bootlace-worm (ribbon-worm or nemertean), which lives on the seashore. Some estimates put its length at more than 98 ft (30 m), but it's only as thick as a little finger. This wriggling predator loops and coils itself under stones, and it can turn its guts inside out in self-defense.

Water Pistols Sea-squirts are simple creatures with leathery, bag-like bodies that stick to rocks and filter water for food. They have no proper eyes, brain, or limbs. Yet they are probably the ancestors of all vertebrate (back-boned) animals, from fish to humans. If prodded when the tide is out they squirt out water.

Bags of Water Jellyfish consist of more than 95 percent water. They have no bones, heart, brain, or real eyes.

Slow Assassin The deadly snail inside a coneshell can jab a small venom-loaded "dart" into your skin. The pain has been described as "red-hot needles being twisted through the veins."

Mudskippers prefer to swim with their 360° swivelling eyes above water. On land they keep them moist by retracting them into water that is stored at the bottom of the eye sockets.

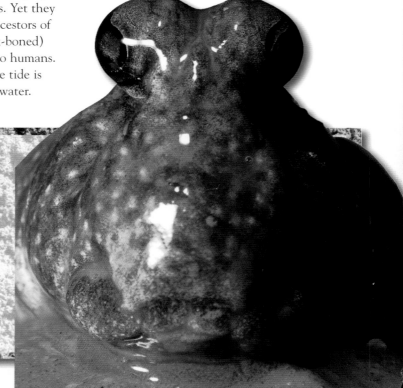

Skipping a Breath

Mudskippers can stay out of water for a day or more, by breathing in three different ways. They carry a small "personal pond" of water inside their large neck gill chambers, from which they absorb oxygen as usual, and which is "refreshed" by dipping into a puddle now and then. They also take in oxygen through their tough, slimy skin. And last, the mouth gapes to absorb oxygen through its blood-rich lining. Mudskippers skip along using their pectoral (front) fins as stumpy legs, and with a tail-flick they can leap a distance of 3 ft (1 m) or more.

Vampire bats make small cuts with their sharp teeth, sucking blood from victims while they are asleep. Special chemicals in their saliva stops the blood from clotting.

Rocky Horrors

As many as ten million bats hang from the roofs of single caves in North America and Indonesia during daylight hours. Their droppings form huge, stinking, slimy mounds of guano, which feeds birds, insects, and other swarming life forms that share the almost total darkness.

BOTTOM FIVE
CAVE DWELLERS

Some animals live deep below the surface of the Earth, depending on water on the cave walls to wash down food from lakes on the surface.

1 **Eyeless shrimps and crayfish**

2 **Blind cave-fish**

3 **Cave crickets**

4 **Cavern salamanders**

5 **White wingless beetles and crickets**

This amazing two-headed American rat snake hatched at an animal park in Tilburg, the Netherlands, in 2002.

Spittle for the Soup

Cave swiftlets of Southeast Asia nest in the ceilings of great caverns. They make their nests from their own saliva, or spit, which dries as a glassy solidified goo, glued to the cavern rock. People use ladders to reach and collect the nests, which are made into the culinary delicacy bird's nest soup. The essence of this dish is therefore swiftlet spit!

Collecting nests for bird's nest soup in Payanak Cave, on Ko Phi Phi Island, Thailand.

Dribble Trap Fungus-gnat grubs in New Zealand cave roofs dribble slime as sticky threads that hang down, then light up their bodies like glow-worms. Small flies are drawn to the light, get trapped in the slimy "web," and the grub hauls them in to eat.

The large African bullfrog can remain underground for a long time, sometimes as long as several years, in the absence of heavy rain. When underground it forms a cocoon that helps to stop water loss. It feeds on other frogs as well as insects and worms.

Roach Hotel The cave cockroach lives its entire life on and in guano—bat droppings on the cavern floor. The cockroaches mate and lay their eggs there, feeding solely on the guano.

Feeling its Way Some kinds of cave cricket have antennae (feelers) ten times longer than their body. The antennae are used not only for touch, but taste and smell too. The cave cricket has no eyes, so if the antennae are damaged, it is doomed.

Hard to Swallow The world's biggest earthworms live in South Africa and Southern Australia. These giants are more than 16 ft (5 m) long when extended and as thick as a wrist when contracted. Their tunnels are so big and slimy that as the worms slide through them, they make gurgling noises audible 300 ft (100 m) away. Toads and birds that try to eat these worms partly swallow one end, and then choke and die as the worm wriggles away unharmed.

Dropping Clues In Australia, a wombat's tunnel entrance can be recognized by its large size, and also by its distinctive droppings nearby, which are cube- or brick-shaped.

Dark Lives Cave fish live their whole life in caves. Because of this they are pale and blind—some have no eyes at all!

Lurking in the Swamps

The huge, saltwater crocodile is the biggest and deadliest reptile, possibly killing as many as ten people each year. Exact numbers of victims are not known since some bodies are never recovered.

Saltwater crocodiles grow to over 23 ft (7 m) long and weight over 1 ton! On hot days they bask on the bank of rivers with their mouths wide open. This stops them from overheating and allows birds to remove parasites and bits of food stuck in their teeth.

SWAMPY FACTS

- Prehistoric crocodiles grew to over 50 ft (15 m) long
- The teeth of alligators amazingly have no roots!
- Alligators, like all reptiles, drown if they are held under water
- Alligators can go without food for up to a year

The saltwater crocodile's varied diet consists of fish, turtles, snakes, birds, buffalo, wild boar, and even monkeys!

CROC SHUTS DOWN MOTORS

In the 1970s in northern Australia, an 18 ft (5.5 m) saltwater croc nicknamed Sweetheart attacked boats and chewed up more than 20 outboard motors—but no people. Its stuffed body is displayed in Darwin Museum.

One in the Eye On Ossabaw Island, Georgia, a biologist was making alligator grunts and splashing his hand in the water, when a huge alligator reared up right in front of him and grabbed his arm. He poked its eye with his other hand and escaped with minor injuries.

Baby white alligators are rare and often suffer from sunburn in the wild.

River Tusker

The male hippo has massive, tusk-like lower canine teeth that can grow to more than 16 in (40 cm) long. When two of these 1.5-ton monsters battle for control of a stretch of river, they can inflict terrible, and even fatal, wounds or may lunge at nearby boats and tip them over.

A hippo's skin sweats an oily red fluid to keep the skin healthy. People used to think that hippos sweated blood!

Low Toll Down Under In Australia you are as likely to be killed by a crocodile as by a shark—about one death yearly, compared to two from lightning, 300 from drowning, and nearly 1,000 from road accidents.

Mugged at Water's Edge The Indian crocodile called the mugger is now feared more than the tiger in some places. It swims into drainage ditches and channels, and grabs people as they come to fill water buckets for their farm animals.

People Make Me Sick! In 1956 a man near Manaus, Brazil, told how he came upon his six-year-old son almost swallowed by a massive anaconda. He hit the snake with an oar so that it coughed up the boy—still alive.

River's Tiny Killers Far more deadly in water than crocs or giant snakes are small parasitic animals such as flukes, worms, and leeches. They spread diseases such as river blindness and elephantiasis, which disfigure and kill hundreds of thousands of people yearly across the tropics.

Tongue Trap The alligator snapping turtle catches fish when they seize its tongue—which they mistake for a worm.

Paralyzing Toad North America's most poisonous toad is the Colorado River toad. Its venom can cause slurred speech, paralysis, and even death.

Walking on Water The basilisk lizard can run along the surface of the water on a lake or pond for up to 400 yds (400 m).

Dry Spell The African lungfish can survive for up to four years embedded beneath the dry lake bed!

Anglers Snakes in the mountains of Valais, Switzerland, lie on the shores of mountain streams and seize trout when they leap above the water.

Fasting A boa constrictor can go without food for a whole year!

Snappy Meal In 1963 a 26-ft (8-m) anaconda was shot in Trinidad and opened to reveal a 5-ft (1.5-m) alligator in its stomach.

Sneaky Sleeper A snake can sleep with both eyes open!

Kantima Pinchai is one of the brave performers at the Sriracha Tiger Farm in Thailand. She stunned audiences when she placed her head inside the jaws of this crocodile, which can crush with a force of over 2,000 lb per sq inch!

Ripley's®
GIANT PYTHON SKIN
EXHIBIT NO: 14127
RED-BALL PYTHON 15 FT (4.5 M)
IN LENGTH

Pythons are known to wander through Singapore's sewer system. Some have appeared in toilets and have been known to bite!

TOO BIG TO HANDLE

The world's bulkiest snake is the anaconda of South America and the Caribbean. It may grow up to 33 ft (10 m) and weigh up to 660 lbs (300 kg). Past tales of giants like an anaconda in the 1940s measuring 130 ft (40 m) and 5 tons are legendary.

Viper Crossing A highway in Shawnee National Forest, Illinois, is closed to automobiles for several weeks twice each year so that it can be crossed safely by copperheads, rattlesnakes, and water moccasins.

Quake Alert Just before an earthquake struck China in 1975, hundreds of hibernating snakes mysteriously emerged from below the ground.

Frozen Solid Garter snakes endure the cold by dropping their heart rates and allowing their bones to freeze solid.

Mouthful! A 16-ft (5-m) long African rock python was once seen swallowing an entire 130 lb (60 kg) impala—horns and all!

Dudu Mia, Bangladeshi snake-charmer, eats some of the 3,500 baby snakes he captured in Bangladesh on April 29, 2002. He claimed to have eaten most of them after capturing them over two days from two houses.

RECYCLED BABIES

Small pregnant desert rodents such as gerbils and jerboas "recycle" their unborn fetuses by absorbing their babies' tissues back into their own bodies. They do this if conditions turn harsh and their offspring are unlikely to survive. If the babies are already born, they eat them instead.

Fat Store When well fed, the camel's hump can contain over 80 lb (40 kg) of fat, which, when broken down within the body to yield energy, produces 16 gal (60 l) of water.

Walk like an Egyptian A camel trots and gallops like no other animal. It moves both legs on one side of the body forward at a time, rocking from side to side, in a unique method called "pacing."

Jumpers Australia's red kangaroo, the biggest marsupial, can cover 33 ft (10 m) in one bound and clear a 10-ft (3-m) fence. In severe drought, the males save energy by stopping sperm production.

Waterless Diet A kangaroo-rat obtains one-tenth of the water it needs from the seeds it eats. The other nine-tenths comes from water actually made in its body, as it digests its food.

No Sweat A camel's body temperature can rise from its normal 100 to 104°F (38 to 40°C), to more than 109°F (43°C) at midday to reduce water loss as sweat. At the other extreme, it can drop to as low as 93°F (34°C) on a cold night to save energy and keep warm.

Long Month A group of camels trekked 534 mi (860 km) across North Australia for 34 days without drinking any water.

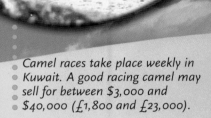

Camel races take place weekly in Kuwait. A good racing camel may sell for between $3,000 and $40,000 (£1,800 and £23,000).

Camels can go without water in the cool season for five months, losing up to 40 percent of their body weight in moisture (humans are near death after losing 12 percent). Then they can drink 32 gal (120 l) of water at 3 gal (12 l) a minute —equivalent to a 2-pt (1-l) juice carton every five seconds for ten minutes!

"camels can trek across blazing hot deserts without drinking any water for over a month"

TOP FIVE
SPRINTERS

Many deserts are wide open stretches of land, so speed is vital to escape enemies or catch prey. These distances show the number of feet and meters traveled in one second.

1 **Cheetah 29 ft (8.8 m)**

2 **Ostrich 21 ft (6.4 m)**

3 **Red kangaroo 14 ft (4.3 m)**

4 **Champion human sprinter 11 ft (3.3 m)**

5 **Dromedary (camel) 9 ft (2.7 m)**

Bladder Supply The water-holding frog of Australia spends more than nine-tenths of its life underground in a skin-like bag waiting for rain so it can dig to the surface, feed, and breed. While buried, up to half of its body weight is very weak urine in its bladder, which is slowly recycled to provide its water needs.

Heavy Hoarder! The North American kangaroo-rat gathers seeds up to 1,000 times its own body weight in its burrow. That's the same as a person filling a 60-ton truck with food!

Praying for Rain The Couch's spadefoot toad, which lives in North America's Sonora Desert, stays underground for 11 months each year, coming up to the surface only during the rainy season in July.

Deep Diggers Ants in the Atacama Desert, Chile, dig deep underground passages 10 ft (3 m) below the surface to reach underground streams.

Beware! The gila monster and the Mexican beaded lizard are the world's only two poisonous lizards.

Venomous Small North African desert scorpions such as the yellow, fat-tailed, buthus and the death-stalker don't need size and strength to subdue prey—they use powerful poison from their arched tail-tip sting. Healthy adult humans usually survive despite many hours of agonizing pain, but old, young, sick, or weak people may die, usually after about seven hours.

Legless The glass lizard has no legs, and at times no tail! The tail breaks off and wriggles as a decoy if attacked.

In Australia a thirsty moloch or thorny devil, a spiky lizard, dips its tail in a puddle and the tiny grooves on its scales allow the water to seep by capillary action, all the way along its body to its mouth.

SHAPELY BLOOD CELLS
The microscopic red blood cells of camels are oval—all other mammals have rounded, saucer-shaped ones.

On average, one person is killed each day in Tunisia from a scorpion sting! The North African country consists mainly of the Sahara Desert and is home to millions of these creatures.

TOP FIVE
DEADLIEST SPIDERS

1 **Sydney funnelweb, Australia**

2 **Black widow, Africa**

3 **Redback, Australia**

4 **Banana spider, North America**

5 **Brown recluse (fiddleback or violin spider), North America**

Poor Guests Many different kinds of woodwasps sting and paralyze caterpillars, lay their eggs inside them, and bury them in soil. The wasp grubs hatch and eat their caterpillar "hosts" alive from the inside out.

On the March The army ants of South America and driver ants of Africa have devoured babies left in cots. They march in columns more than one million strong. Small animals that cannot get out the way are stung to death and torn apart for food by thousands of tiny pairs of pincers.

Gas Sniffers Turkey buzzards are used to detect gas leaks in pipelines in southern California!

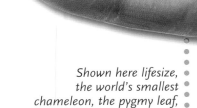

Shown here lifesize, the world's smallest chameleon, the pygmy leaf, weighs just 0.1 oz (3 g).

Leaf Sweeper After a big feed, more than one-third of the weight of a proboscis monkey is the leaves that are jammed into its stomach.

Heavy Meals A large African elephant eats more than 350 lbs (160 kg) of food each day—the weight of two large humans.

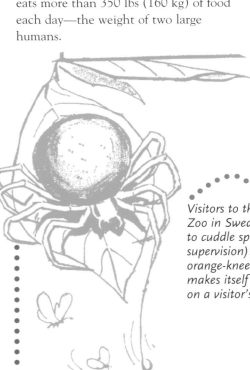

Visitors to the Stockholm Zoo in Sweden are allowed to cuddle spiders (under supervision)! This Mexican orange-kneed bird spider makes itself comfortable on a visitor's face.

The magnificent spider from Australia fishes for food by spinning a fine, silk line 1.5 in (4 cm) long. It uses a sticky globule at the end as bait and its foreleg as the casting rod.

Eight-leg Giants

The largest spider is the Goliath bird-eating tarantula of South America. With leg spans of almost 12 in (30 cm) it would cover your dinner plate. Slightly smaller but heavier is the Salmon Pink bird-eater, also of South America, weighing over 3 oz (80 g). A Salmon Pink ate two frogs and two young snakes in four days, then slept for two weeks.

Tarantulas hunt at night, feasting on animals such as frogs, birds, and lizards. They crush prey with their large fangs.

This amazing colored snake, the eyelash pit viper, has long fangs with which to lunge at prey, mouth open, piercing fur and feathers to inject a deadly venom.

Quick Charge! Despite weighing more than 5 tons, an African elephant can run faster than a human champion sprinter, at speeds of over 25 mph (40 km/h).

Heavy Head A big moose's antlers can weigh more than 55 lb (25 kg). That's like having an eight-year-old child strapped to your head!

Population Explosion If a common housefly mated and laid 500 eggs and they all hatched and reproduced, the fly population would increase by about 30,000,000,000,000 each year!

Top Tree-dweller The largest animal that lives its life in trees is the male orang-utan of Southeast Asia, which can weigh more than 175 lbs (80 kg) —as much as a large human.

Long Life The same black garden ants have been kept in ant-nest tanks for about 20 years. Relative to size, a human that lived for the same time would survive for 10 billion years!

Hard Lesson to Learn A scientist saw a mother chimp teach her youngster to break open nuts by hitting them with a stone. When the youngster got bored and looked away, she gave him a slap and made him watch again!

The sticky tongue of this Picasso Panther chameleon can extend up to one and a half times its body length to catch a cricket—then return back into its mouth in a tenth of a second!

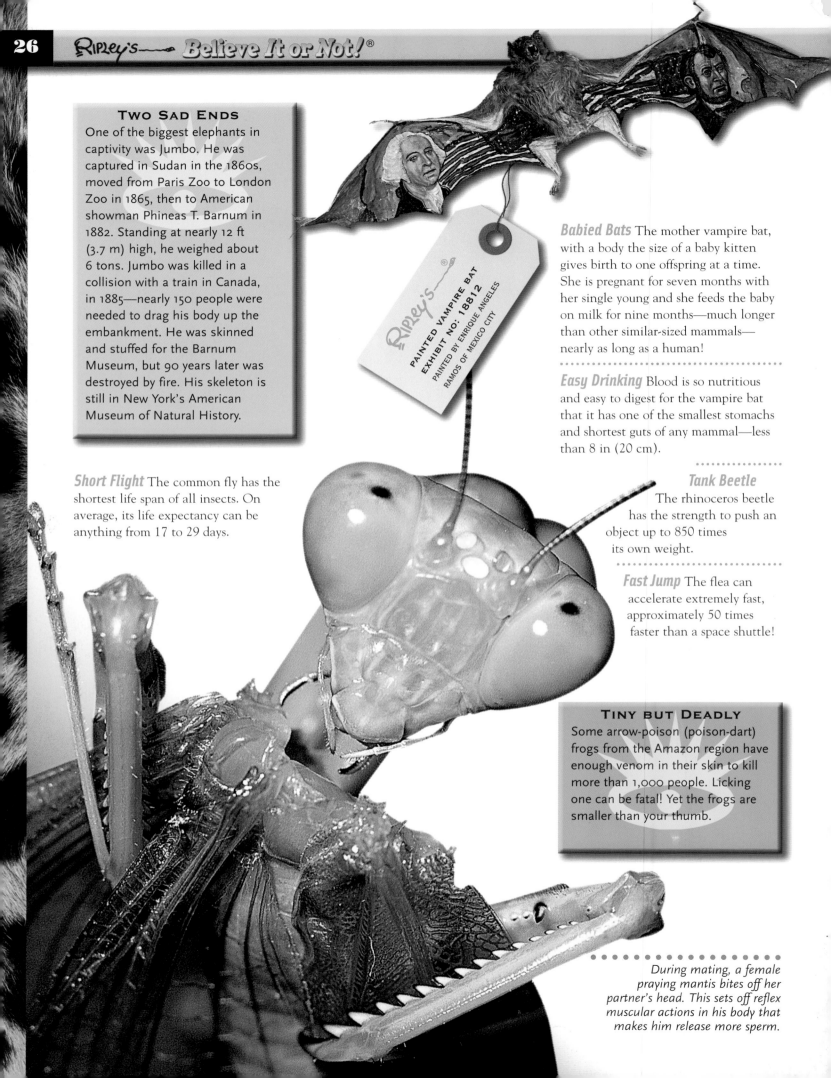

TWO SAD ENDS

One of the biggest elephants in captivity was Jumbo. He was captured in Sudan in the 1860s, moved from Paris Zoo to London Zoo in 1865, then to American showman Phineas T. Barnum in 1882. Standing at nearly 12 ft (3.7 m) high, he weighed about 6 tons. Jumbo was killed in a collision with a train in Canada, in 1885—nearly 150 people were needed to drag his body up the embankment. He was skinned and stuffed for the Barnum Museum, but 90 years later was destroyed by fire. His skeleton is still in New York's American Museum of Natural History.

Ripley's® PAINTED VAMPIRE BAT EXHIBIT NO: 18812 PAINTED BY ENRIQUE ANGELES RAMOS OF MEXICO CITY

Babied Bats The mother vampire bat, with a body the size of a baby kitten gives birth to one offspring at a time. She is pregnant for seven months with her single young and she feeds the baby on milk for nine months—much longer than other similar-sized mammals— nearly as long as a human!

Easy Drinking Blood is so nutritious and easy to digest for the vampire bat that it has one of the smallest stomachs and shortest guts of any mammal—less than 8 in (20 cm).

Short Flight The common fly has the shortest life span of all insects. On average, its life expectancy can be anything from 17 to 29 days.

Tank Beetle The rhinoceros beetle has the strength to push an object up to 850 times its own weight.

Fast Jump The flea can accelerate extremely fast, approximately 50 times faster than a space shuttle!

TINY BUT DEADLY

Some arrow-poison (poison-dart) frogs from the Amazon region have enough venom in their skin to kill more than 1,000 people. Licking one can be fatal! Yet the frogs are smaller than your thumb.

During mating, a female praying mantis bites off her partner's head. This sets off reflex muscular actions in his body that makes him release more sperm.

It's a Leopard's Life

CAT-A-LOG

- Leopards have unique spot patterns, just like humans have fingerprints

- Tigers do not just have striped fur, they have striped skin, too!

- From a standing start, a cheetah can reach a speed of 62 mph (100 km/h) in just three seconds

- The heaviest recorded tiger weighed in at 1,025 lbs (465 kg)

- A snow leopard can leap a distance of 50 ft (15 m)

- Lions spend more than 20 hours resting a day

Known as the Leopard Man of Skye, Tom Leppard from Scotland has had the whole of his body tattooed in the markings of a big cat. For almost 15 years Leopard Man has lived in a hut made from sticks and stones, on a part of the island that is only reachable by boat and a two-hour hike.

Leopard Man bathes himself in the river and travels by canoe to pick up supplies and his pension once a week. He declares that he has everything he needs and is never lonely.

Leopard Man has had more than 99 percent of his body tattooed—only the skin between his toes and the insides of his ears remain untouched!

Leopards can grow to a weight of 200 lbs (90 kg). They are thought to be twice as strong as a human and can drag a carcass weighing 600 lb (270 kg)—the weight of four average-size human beings—20 ft (6 m) up into a tree to feed!

Entombed in Ice

A 23-ton block of ice containing the remains of a 20,380-year-old male wooly mammoth was discovered in the summer of 1997 by nine-year-old Simion Jarkov near Khatanga, on the Taimyr Peninsula.

French explorer Bernard Buigues arrived on the scene and dug down, with a plan to excavate the entire mammoth. This involved digging the mammoth out, still contained in the block of ice and transporting it by air to a frozen cave. Here, plans were made to thaw out the ice slowly with hairdryers. After just three days, he found the mammoth's skull! But as he dug deeper he discovered the mammoth bones were without flesh. Buigues' idea to clone the wooly mammoth failed.

FREE-FALL

In 1997 an Austrian mountain-rescue climber saw an alpine ibex stumble, bounce, and fall down a huge cliff, pick itself up at the base and walk away. The climber later checked the height of the cliff with a laser tape-measure. It was almost 3,200 ft (1,000 m) high.

Bat keeps it Cool A big brown bat "hibernated" in a laboratory fridge at just above freezing for 344 days— more than 11 months.

King Cat The Siberian tiger is the biggest tiger and the largest of all cats, with a head to body length exceeding 8.5 ft (2.6 m) and a weight of 660-plus lbs (300-plus kg). It is also the most northerly and the rarest kind of tiger, living in snowy north-east Asia. There are probably fewer than 200 left.

Bernard Buigues examining the wooly mammoth tusks in northern Siberia, hopeful that the permafrost below contained the fully preserved body of a wooly mammoth.

TOP FIVE
COLD-SURVIVORS

Some species can cope with extreme weather conditions.

1 **Arctic fox** can survive for days at −22°F (−30°C) if well-fed

2 **Musk ox of North America** has longest hair of any mammal at up to 3 ft (1 m)

3 **Yak of the Himalayas, central Asia** survives on ice-fields at 20,000 ft (6,000 m)

4 **Ptarmigan** can survive sub-zero temperatures for six weeks

5 **Snow bunting** nests nearer to the North Pole than any other bird

Pale Prospects Albino or white types are known for most animals, from frogs and snakes to bison, tigers, gorillas, and whales—even albino polar bears! The lack of color is caused by a genetic change or mutation. In the wild, apart from ice and snowy places, albino animals stand out so clearly that they rarely survive long. For example, albino tigers are easily visible to prey as they stalk through undergrowth. It's thought that about one tiger in 10,000 is born nearly or completely white.

Highest Predator The snow leopard is found higher than any other big hunting animal, more than 16,400 ft (5,000 m) up in the Himalayas.

Heavy Sleepers Rodents such as marmots and birch mice in Siberia hibernate in burrows for up to eight months of the year.

Hairy Insulation The musk ox, which lives in the freezing, dry lands of the Arctic, has such a long, thick, and wooly undercoat that when the creature lies down to rest, its body heat does not melt the snow beneath it.

Cold Storage Wood frogs, spring peepers, and several other amphibians thaw out alive and completely unharmed after being almost totally frozen for more than three months of each year.

"tigers can eat 110 lb of meat at a time"

A big, hungry tiger can eat almost 110 lb (50 kg) of meat in one meal—equivalent to an average person consuming 50-plus half-pounder burgers.

Sleeping with Scorpions

In 2002 Kanchana Ketkeaw from Thailand made herself at home in a glass box where she remained alone for 32 days with just 3,400 scorpions for company! She was allowed to leave the box for 15 minutes every eight hours.

During this marathon stay Kanchana was stung nine times! Some scorpions died during her ordeal, others gave birth, and some extras were added to keep the numbers constant. Each day she fed them on raw egg and ground pork. Kanchana performs with scorpions every day at a local tourist attraction, part of her act involves placing the animals in her mouth. She has been stung hundreds of times—so often, doctors say, that she is probably now immune to scorpion poison.

Unperturbed by their dangerous stings, Kanchana Ketkeaw lives happily among scorpions.

"It was like being in a room at home, only with thousands of little friends"

SIZE COUNTS
Some species of scorpion can grow up to 8.5 in (21 cm) long—as big as a man's hand! These scorpions tend to be less poisonous than the smaller variety that grow up to 4 in (12 cm) in length. A sting from one of these smaller scorpions can cause paralysis.

Termite! The queen white ant (or termite) lays 80,000 eggs a day and is the mother of the entire colony.

Stepping Out If moving our legs at the same rate as an ant, our movement speed would be 800 mph (500 km/h)!

Longest Insect The giant stick insect from Indonesia can grow to an amazing length—up to 13 in (33 cm).

New Bugs Nearly 1,000 insect species are discovered every year.

Lethal Bee The honeybee kills more people around the world each year than do all the poisonous snakes in the world put together.

Steep Crawlers Some insects are able to climb walls and even windows. This is because they have feet with tiny hooks or sticky pads.

Sweet Tooth The aborigines of Australia dig up the nests of honey ants and eat the insects.

Crunchy Snacks!

In Phnom Penh's central market in Cambodia, stalls sell grilled insects and spiders! Hairy tarantulas, which are as big as your hand, are a very popular snack served during the day. Fried worms in Bangkok, Thailand, are threaded onto skewers. In China, small scorpions are considered a delicacy. They are cooked using garlic, herbs, and other spices to enhance the flavor.

Tiny bedbugs feed on human blood. Once well-fed, they can survive for six months before they need to feed again.

High-rise Nest The paper nest of the Brazilian wasp looks and swings like a Japanese lantern, but is actually like a miniature skyscraper. It is made up of at least 20 or more storys.

Air Miles A monarch butterfly can fly 620 mi (995 km) without even stopping to eat!

Nosy Insect An ant has five noses, each of which has a different task to perform.

Sleeping Beauty Snails can sleep for long periods of time—up to three years!

An unusual delicacy—a plate of worms! These creatures are fried and sold by street vendors in Thailand to those who have developed a taste for such a dish!

The high jump champion of the insect world is the froghopper. It can easily jump higher than an Olympic high jump champion! It is only 0.1 in (3 mm) in length but can jump to a height of 27 in (70 cm). If human beings were able to jump as high, they could clear a 650 ft (200 m) building!

TOP FIVE
SOARING BIRDS

1 **Alpine choughs 28,000 ft (8,500 m), Himalayas**

2 **Whooper swans 27,000 ft (8,200 m), northern Britain**

3 **Bar-headed geese over 26,000 ft (8,000 m), Himalayas**

4 **Steppe eagle 26,000 ft (7,900 m), Himalayas**

5 **Bearded vulture 23,000 ft (7,000 m), Himalayas**

Love Struck Swan A male swan in Hamburg, Germany, fell in love with a swan-shaped pedal boat. Every time someone went near the boat, the swan went wild with jealousy!

HIGHEST STRIKE

In 1962 the crew of a U.S. Electra-188 airliner heard a thud to the rear of the airplane at a height of 21,000 ft (6,400 m) over Nevada. On landing, blood and feather remains on the tailplane were identified as those of a common duck, the mallard.

Birds are Best Birds can fly far higher than bats since their lungs take in up to three times more oxygen than bat lungs. At heights approaching 32,000 ft (10,000 m), there's only two-fifths of the oxygen that is in the air at sea level. Also, the temperature of the air is below –40°F (–40°C).

Bugs on High Butterflies called queen of Spain fritillaries and small tortoiseshells have been seen actively flying (rather than storm-blown) at 20,000 ft (6,000 m).

Deadly Dive The fastest of all animals is the peregrine falcon. When seeking prey, it reaches speeds of more than 150 mph (240 km/h) in its "power-dive" called a stoop, as it swoops down in mid-air to catch a bird.

Top Flight Meals Mexican free-tailed bats have recently been tracked by radar higher than 10,000 ft (3,000 m) above Texas. Millions leave caves at dusk to eat migrating moths, mainly at heights of 2,000 to 3,200 ft (600 to 1,000 m).

Eating on the Fly The great skua harasses other birds that are flying back from feeding trips over the ocean and makes them disgorge partly-digested food, which the skua catches and eats in mid air.

HIGH FLYERS

- *Concorde* was able to cruise at 59,000 ft (18,000 m)
- Most modern jet passenger planes cruise at 30,000 to 33,000 ft (9,000 to 10,000 m)
- Highest birds fly 28,000-plus ft (8,500-plus m)
- Cirrus clouds (the highest common type) form at 26,000 ft (8,000 m)

Moth cocoons can be unbelievably massive— they can sometimes cover an entire tree.

SPACE ZOO

In 1998 a space shuttle took up "Neurolab," a package of various animals that were tested and studied to gauge their reactions to conditions in space. There were 1,500 crickets, 230 swordtail fish, 130 water snails, 150 rats, and 18 pregnant mice. The swordtail fish, crickets, and water snails were dissected on their return to Earth, to study how their gravity-detecting balance sensors had reacted to weightless conditions. This work is aimed at helping people with certain kinds of deafness that affect the ear's inner hearing and balance sensors.

Shuttle Survivors Canisters of tiny roundworms (nematodes) were the only living survivors of the *Columbia* shuttle disaster on February 1, 2003. As the craft burned up on re-entry, a shuttle mid-deck locker housing the worms' canister was thrown free and fell to Earth in eastern Texas.

Wonky Webs Spiders were taken up to the Skylab space station in the 1970s, where they spun very crooked, untidy webs. Eight garden orb-web spiders provided by a school in Melbourne, Florida, were on the ill-fated *Columbia* shuttle trip in February 2003.

Growth Tests In 1990, 16 laboratory rats were given a growth hormone during a shuttle trip, to see which parts of their bodies grew, and how fast, in weightless conditions. It was part of tests for a new GM form of growth hormone.

Bio-satellites Animal astronauts in the 1970s to 1990s, aboard the seven Russian Cosmos biological satellites, included over 100 rats and fruit flies used for genetic studies, each carrying eight rhesus monkeys. The only problems affecting the fruit flies were "difficulty in mating in zero G."

Ham, the first astro-chimp, tested life-support conditions aboard a U.S. Mercury space mission in 1961, and came back safely.

Space Victims In the late 1950s an estimated 13 dogs and four monkeys died before space scientists were able to bring animals back alive from space.

Panic of First Space Trip

A Russian dog named Laika, captured as a stray in Moscow, took off in *Sputnik 2* in November 1957. Officials said she survived for several days and was then painlessly put to sleep. In 2002, however, new evidence showed that she died after just a few hours, of overheating, panic, and stress. Her *Sputnik* "coffin" continued on 2,570 orbits and burned up during re-entry as a "shooting star" as it fell back to Earth in April 1958.

Laika, the first animal in space, orbited the Earth at an altitude of nearly 2,000 mi (3,200 km).

Index

Index

ACKNOWLEDGMENTS

Jacket (t/r) Digital Vision

6 (c) Gregory Ochocki/Seapics.com; 7 (t) Kay Nietfield/AFP/GETTYIMAGE, (b/r) STF/AFP/GETTYIMAGE; 8 (t) Doc White/Seapics.com, (b) Matthias Schrader/AFP/GETTYIMAGE; 9 (b/r) Universal, (b) Amos Nachoum/CORBIS, 10 (r) Jeffrey L. Rotman/CORBIS, (b) Jeffrey L. Rotman/CORBIS; 11 (r) Royalty-Free/CORBIS; 12 (t) Tom Brakefield/CORBIS, (b) Galen Rowell/CORBIS; 13 (c) Jeffrey L. Rotman/CORBIS; 14 (t) Roger Garwood & Trish Ainslie/CORBIS (b) Paul A. Souders/CORBIS; 16 (b) Martin Harvey, Gallo Images/CORBIS; 17 (t) Michael and Patricia Fogden/Corbis; 18 (t/l) Robin Utrecht/AFP/GETTYIMAGE, (t/r) Michael Freeman.CORBIS, (b) Joe McDonald/CORBIS; 19 (t) Martin Harvey, Gallo Images/CORBIS; 20 Background STT/AFP/GETTYIMAGE, (b) Pornchai Kittiwongsakul/AFP/GETTYIMAGE; 21 (t) INS News Group/REX, (b) Mohammad Ibrahim/AFP/GETTYIMAGE; 22 (t) Raed Qutena/AFP/GETTYIMAGE, (b) Jim Erickson/CORBIS; 24 (t) Yoshikazu Tsuno/AFP/GETTYIMAGE, (b) Gunner Ask/AFP/GETTYIMAGE; 25 (c/l) David A. Northcott/CORBIS, (b) Paul J. Richards/AFP/GETTYIMAGE; 27 (c) Tom Kidd/Katz; 28 (b) AFP/GETTYIMAGE; 29 (b) Keren Su/CORBIS; 31 (t/l) AFP/GETTYIMAGE (b) Roger Wilmhurst, FLPA/CORBIS, (t/r) SAM YEH/AFP/GETTYIMAGE; 32 (b) Action Press/REX; 33 (t) Courtesy of NASA, (b) AFP/GETTYIMAGE;

All other photos are from Corel, PhotoDisc, Digital Vision and Ripley's Entertainment Inc.